WHEN John Wayne vaults his two hundred pound, six foot three inch frame into the saddle, he does so with a rare authority! On his father's ranch near the edge of the Mojave Desert, young Wayne learned to ride almost before he could walk. His huge and rugged frame enabled him to excel at most sports, but best of all he loved to swim in the huge irrigation ditch near the ranch.

When John reached high school, he immediately became interested in organized sports, and soon became outstanding in all fields, particularly football, where his speed and power marked him as an outstanding prospect for college football. Although his ambition was to go to Annapolis, he faced disappointment in being beaten by only one man in a competitive test. Instead he entered the University of Southern California, where he became a star football player.

During his first college vacation, John Wayne decided to see the world. Being a man of direct action—and limited funds—he stowed away on a Honolulu bound freighter fortified with three sandwiches and a couple of candy bars! They found him asleep in a lifeboat on the third day out. Instead of locking him up, they put the husky lad to work.

After graduation, he got a job driving a truck at a movie studio. Here he was discovered by a movie director, and once he climbed back into chaps and spurs, he's had little time for anything else. John went on to become one of the outstanding western stars of the day. He joins the publishers in hoping you really get a whack out of this magazine!

DON'T MISS
JOHN WAYNE IN
"SHE WORE A YELLOW RIBBON"
AN ARGOSY PICTURE
PRODUCED AND DIRECTED BY
JOHN FORD

JOHN WAYNE ADVENTURE COMICS, NO. 1, Winter Issue. Published by TOBY PRESS, INC., 17 East 45th Street, New York 17, N. Y. Single Copies, 10 cents, Copyright 1949, by Toby Press, Inc. Printed in the U.S.A. The stories, names, characters, incidents, and institutions mentioned or portrayed in this periodical, excepting those who have authorized the use of their names herein, are entirely imaginary

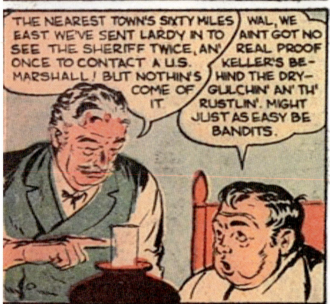

WAYNE in The Mysterious Valley of Violence

IN A BIZARRE ATMOSPHERE OF GLOOM AND MYSTERY STANDS THAT STRUCTURE KNOWN AS "NERO'S CASTLE." FOR YEARS, COWBOYS AND TRAVELLERS HAD GIVEN IT A WIDE BERTH, AND EVEN THE HARDIEST OF ADVENTURERS SHUDDERED AND LOWERED THEIR VOICES AS THEY SPOKE OF THE MYSTERIOUS MASTER OF "NERO LAND." IT IS HERE THAT JOHN WAYNE ENCOUNTERED ONE OF THE STRANGEST ADVENTURES OF HIS CAREER.

"I GOT 'EM ALL, JOHN, 'CEPT A COUPLE OF DOGGIES ESCAPED DOWN THAT NARROW CANYON."

"WELL, I'M GOING ALONG AFTER THEM!"

"DON'T JOHN, I TELL YOU DON'T!"

JOHN'S SENSES, SHARPENED BY YEARS OF DANGEROUS LIVING, WARNS HIM OF THE NEARBY SAGEBRUSH.

SHOULD YOU DOUBT MY WORD, MR. WAYNE, MERELY MAKE THE SLIGHTEST MOVE TOWARD YOUR GUN!

--AND HE SEES

ALL RIGHT, MISTER, THIS ROUND BELONGS TO YOU!

SMARTLY DONE, MR. WAYNE, SMARTLY DONE. YOU PROBABLY REASON AS I DO THAT DYING THIS WAY IS SO DULL.

DYING ANY WAY DON'T FIT INTO MY PLANS, MR.---

NERO'S THE NAME, SON.

SUDDENLY JOHN WAYNE SPOTS AN OPENING IN THE UNDERBRUSH. WITH THE SPEED OF A PANTHER, HE MAKES HIS PLAY FOR FREEDOM.

"YIPPEE!! I GOT ME A BIG ONE!"

"YOU'LL STAND TRIAL, MR. NERO, AND I HOPE THE GRAND JURY GETS A GOOD PICTURE OF THE TYPE OF MAN YOU REALLY ARE. WHY WHEN PETE AND I TESTIFY--"

"CORRECTION, WAYNE-- PETE JAMES AIN'T SETTING FOOT INTO NO COMBINATION COURT- HOUSE AND JAIL... TOO MANY FOLKS MIGHT LIKE TO DE- TAIN ME FOR A WHILE -- SAY TEN YEARS!"

"ADIOS, WAYNE -- AND I'M CONFESSIN' THAT IF THE BULLETS IN THEM SIX- SHOOTERS WAS SHOT IN ANGER INSTEAD OF INTA THE AIR -- IDA BEEN BETTIN' ON WAYNE INSTEAD O' PETE JAMES!"

"GOOD-BYE, PETE, AND GOOD LUCK!"

Starry Night Publishing

Everyone has a story...

Don't spend your life trying to get published! Don't tolerate rejection! Don't do all the work and allow the publishing companies reap the rewards!

Millions of independent authors like you, are making money, publishing their stories now. Our technological know-how will take the headaches out of getting published. Let "Starry Night Publishing.Com" take care of the hard parts, so you can focus on writing. You simply send us your Word Document and we do the rest. It really is that simple!

The big companies want to publish only "celebrity authors," not the average book-writer. It's almost impossible for first-time authors to get published today. This has led many authors to go the self-publishing route. Until recently, this was considered "vanity-publishing." You spent large sums of your money, to get twenty copies of your book, to give to relatives at Christmas, just so you could see your name on the cover. Now, however, the self-publishing industry allows authors to get published in a timely fashion, retain the rights to your work, keeping up to ninety-percent of your royalties, instead of the traditional five-percent.

We've opened up the gates, allowing you inside the world of publishing. While others charge you as much as fifteen-thousand dollars for a publishing package, we charge less than five-hundred dollars to cover copyright, ISBN, and distribution costs. Do you really want to spend all your time formatting, converting, designing a cover, and then promoting your book, because no one else will?

Our editors are professionals, able to create a top-notch book that you will be proud of. Becoming a published author is supposed to be fun, not a hassle.

At Starry Night Publishing, you submit your work, we create a professional-looking cover, a table of contents, compile your text and images into the appropriate format, convert your files for eReaders, take care of copyright information, assign an ISBN, allow you to keep one-hundred-percent of your rights, distribute your story worldwide on Amazon, Barnes & Noble and many other retailers, and write you a check for your royalties. There are no other hidden fees involved! You don't pay extra for a cover, or to keep your book in print. We promise! Everything is included! You even get a free copy of your book and unlimited half-price copies.

In four short years, we've published more than fifteen-hundred books, compared to the major publishing houses which only add an average of six new titles per year. We will publish your fiction, or non-fiction books about anything, and look forward to reading your stories and sharing them with the world.

We sincerely hope that you will join the growing Starry Night Publishing family, become a published author and gain the world-wide exposure that you deserve. You deserve to succeed. Success comes to those who make opportunities happen, not those who wait for opportunities to happen. You just have to try. Thanks for joining us on our journey.

www.starrynightpublishing.com

www.facebook.com/starrynightpublishing/

Made in the USA
Monee, IL
16 June 2025